YOU *still* Wouldn't LIKE IT Here

A Guide to the *REAL* Upper Peninsula of Michigan

The Sequel

Lon L. Emerick

From notes by Sam Satterly

with *more* disturbing illustrations
by Carolyn Damstra

ISBN-13: 978-1-892384-44-7
ISBN-10: 1-892384-44-2

Library of Congress Control Number: 2007928581

First Edition 2007

10 9 8 7 6 5 4 3

Published by
Avery Color Studios, Inc.
Gwinn, Michigan 49841

Dedicated to

the Upper Peninsula residents who live in,
love, and protect this special land.

". . . and this place, which some would say is on the edge of nowhere, for me is the center of everywhere."

—Heather Lende
If You Lived Here, I'd Know Your Name
News from Small-Town Alaska

Contents

Illustrations

Prologue

I never thought I would hear again from the mysterious Sam Satterly. My latest book, *You Wouldn't Like It Here: A Guide to the Real Upper Peninsula of Michigan*, was launched, in the autumn of 2005, and almost instantly was a big hit with the residents of the Upper Peninsula. Most Yoopers looked at the cover and started to laugh; when they flipped through the pages and found the map, they smiled broadly and said, "Yep!" followed by that strange, audible inhalation endemic to the region. Some –though not all– individuals from outside the Upper Peninsula often didn't get the humor and looked blankly at the book; a few were offended by the "unfriendly title."

When I leaked to the media that I planned to stand at the north bound lane of the Mackinac Bridge and hand out copies of *You Wouldn't Like It Here* to all prospective visitors, the regional chambers of commerce and tourist bureaus threatened to buy up the entire inventory of books and shred them. Some local merchants put up a photograph of me in the local post office and stuck pins in it. My favorite response to the book was an e-mail from a local realtor challenging me to a "dual."

I thought that I had done my duty to save the Upper Peninsula from becoming a colony for the rich and uncaring.

Imagine my astonishment when, in deep and dark December, a note scribbled on sheets of birch bark appeared in my mailbox.

Sam Satterly was back and clearly he was not pleased. Once again he challenged me: "You got to write a sequel to *You Wouldn't Like It Here* and make the warnings clearer." Periodically throughout the winter of 2006, other notes –some on bathroom parchment– were found nailed to trees or under the windshield wipers of my truck. After a great deal of soul searching, and with considerable reluctance, I decided to accept Satterly's challenge: I would "write it again, Sam."

None of my renewed efforts to determine the identity of Sam Satterly were successful; I concluded that perhaps it is better that he remains an Upper Peninsula mystery.

Lon Emerick
Skandia, Michigan
Summer, 2007

SAM Satterly's LETTER

Hey Emerick,

You put up those "visually impaired hunter" signs on your property! You must think you are pretty clever, eh?

But only them downstate apple-knockers would be afraid to come on your land. Us old time Yoopers would get the humor right off. Anyway, Emerick, I didn't go on your property again or use one of them fancy deer blinds of yours.

Well, I had to buy one of them little green books— and I wrote the bloody thing! I went to a couple of your book signings and you never even knew I was there. Hah, hah. Real charming you are, Emerick, hugging all them women. But if you keep asking the men if they tell their wives they love them at least once a day, you're going to get a knuckle sandwich. What's wrong with you? You know that U.P. husbands don't do mushy stuff like that. Do you want to spoil all the Yooper wives, or what?

Anyway, that book turned out pretty good but you left out too much stuff. It ain't strong enough. They're still coming!

Everywhere I look, them trolls are building fancy trophy homes, with four bathrooms. What the heck is wrong with those people? Why do they need all them bathrooms? Lousy toilet training or what?

You know what really pulled my chain this past summer? This here guy from Grand Rapids bought a 20 acre parcel down the road from me in Skandia Township. No problem there. But then he asked me about building a house there and I told him he might have a problem digging a well in that marshy spot. He looked at me real funny and

DANGER!
visually-impaired
Hunter

asked, "Why would I need a well?" I pointed out, kinda sarcastic-like, that most people like water for drinking, showers and such. Again this sorry pilgrim stared at me for several seconds and said, "No problem. I'll just have the city bring out the water." Holy Waugh! He had no clue that the city of Marquette wouldn't hardly extend a water line out fourteen miles from town!

So, anyway, Emerick, here's the thing you need to make clear: Happiness for us Yoopers is watching a Californian heading south over the Big Mac Bridge with a troll under each arm.

Sam Satterly

CANADA
ISLE ROYALE
LAKE SUPE
FINLAND
WASH
MONT
N.D.
MINN
CALUMET
TOIVOLA
L'ANSE
MARQUETTE
IRONWOOD
MICH
ORE
IDAHO
WYO
S.D.
RIDDLE
IRON RIVER
IRON MOUNTAIN
GLADSTO
ESCANABA
NEV
CALIF
UTAH
EAGLE
NEB
WIS
IOWA
COLO
BIRD CITY
MINA
VALLEJO
LONE PINE
COLUMBUS JCT.
MENOMINEE
MILWAUKEE
KAN
ARIZ
MEDICINE LODGE
BENSON
N. MEX
MO
ILL
CHICA
OKLA
FORT SMITH
ARK
SMACKOVER
MEXICO
TEXAS
PACIFIC OCEAN

The Official..
Map of Michigan
Drawn in Michigan's Upper Peninsula
By Eugene S. Sinervo ~ 1972 ©
MUNISING
NEWBERRY
SOO
EBEN
GAN
RAPID RIVER
MANISTIQUE
ST. IGNACE
GEORGIAN
LAKE HURON
L.P.
PAW PAW
ONTARIO
NIAGARA
LAKE ERIE
EAGLE LAKE
MAINE
NORWAY
VT
NH
NORTH ADAMS
MASS
WORCESTER
HOPE
CONN
NY
NJ
PENN
MD
SNOW HILL
IND
OHIO
W. VA
VA
SANTA CLAUS
PARIS
FORT KNOX
KY
N.C.
TENN
S.C.
GA
JESUP
ALB
SELMA
MISS
TALAHASSE
FLA
NAPLES
BUNKIE
GULF OF MEXICO
ATLANTIC OCEAN

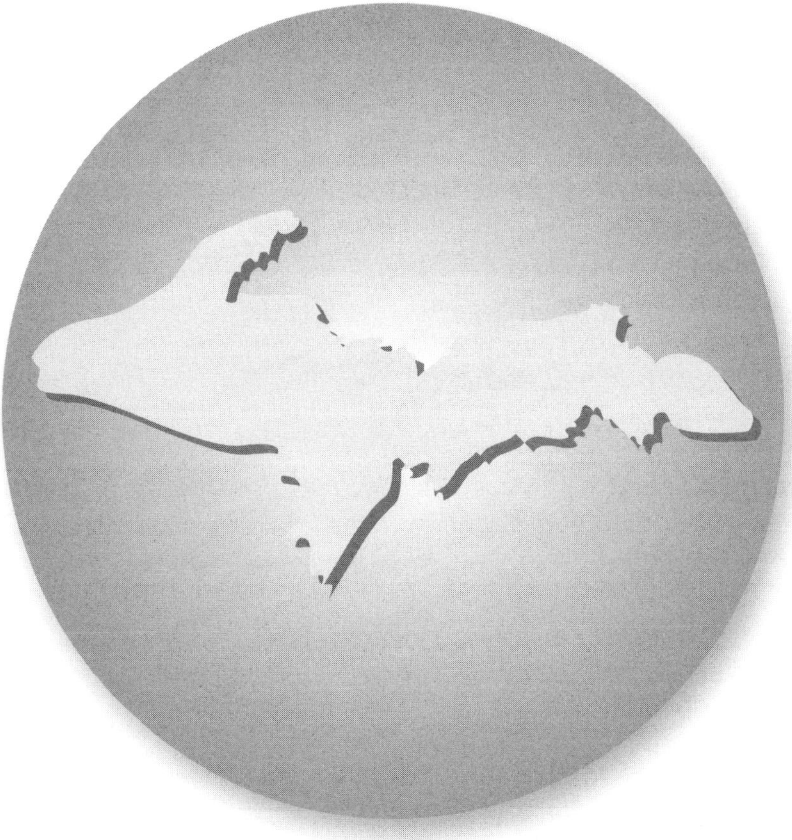

THE Real U.P.

REALLY, YOU WOULDN'T LIKE IT HERE. The tourist bureau prints a ton of slick, colorful brochures about the U.P.

Warning!

This guide is not one of them. You want the truth, right, not a bunch of fables about the mystical UP NORTH? Don't be hoodwinked by promises of fun and fulfillment in the Upper Peninsula–they just want your money and will go to any length to lure you up here. Like that silly (and contradictory) travel bureau advertising slogan, developed by an out-of-state, big city (and expensive) consulting firm: "Discover how civilized our wilderness can be." What a bunch of nonsense.

Even the Founding Fathers knew a dismal, god-for-saken place when they heard about it.

Shortly after the American Revolutionary War, rumors circulated about the immense mineral wealth in Michigan's Upper Peninsula. But most lawmakers expressed doubt that the Lake Superior region would ever be developed. Patrick Henry, he of the "Give me liberty or give me death" speech, was especially caustic. "The entire region," Henry stated, "is beyond the most distant wilderness and remote as the moon." Old Pat got it right, eh?

The U.P. is a forbidding place–dark, endless winters, gloomy forests, hordes of biting insects, fearsome wildlife and desperate human inhabitants. Visiting the Upper Peninsula will be one of the worst mistakes of your life. I can guarantee that once you get here, your entire energy will be devoted to how to flee.

The local residents know all this but cannot or will not leave because they are addicted to suffering. Just consider these names of only a few locations in the U.P.: Misery Bay, Dismal Seepage, Germfask, Pine Stump Junction, Hog Island. Don't those names conjure up beauty and tranquility? Paraphrasing Gertrude Stein, there is no here, here. Why would you want to visit 16,347 square miles of desolation?

The Upper Peninsula is beyond the end of the road. It is far away from any modern civilization, and the residents don't like to follow any of your usual rules. If you want to have a good time on your vacation, don't expect it up here–head for the Wisconsin Dells or Disney World instead.

You probably think I'm exaggerating. Well, let me tell you about what happened last deer season at the Kernow Hunting Camp in Big Bay.

The members of the Kernow Camp are all getting a bit long in the tooth and most of them are nursing various ailments. Instead of hunting alone, they decided to pair up so that if someone had a problem, his partner could summon help. Old Bernie Medlyn, who had been through some heart troubles, was paired with his good buddy, Harvey Treloar, and on opening day they went up to a new deer blind on the Salmon Trout River.

It was almost dark when Harvey struggled back into camp dragging a beautiful eight-point buck. All the old guys ran out of the cabin to admire Harvey's deer. It was the best whitetail buck taken at Kernow Camp in many years and Harvey basked in all the praise and awe. When the excitement had settled down, Alex Pentreath asked, "Say, Harvey, where's Bernie?"

Harvey looked down at his deer and then up at the circle of his longtime hunting buddies. "Well, guys, Bernie got real sick after lunch... and he died," Harvey said. There was a collective audible sigh of shock and disbelief.

"But Harvey," Alex said incredulously, "you dragged this here buck back to camp and left Bernie in the woods?"

Harvey took off his blaze orange Stormy Kromer hat, looked down admiringly at his

Kernow Camp
KC

eight-point buck and replied, "No one's going to steal Bernie." The men looked at each other, nodded in agreement and filed back into the camp to have a celebratory drink to Harvey's successful hunt.

Geography

IN 1835, THE GOVERNOR AND legislators of the Territory of Michigan would have gladly traded the Upper Peninsula for a much smaller strip of land (the Toledo Strip, 470 square miles) on the border with Ohio. In fact, it took a mini-war between the State of Ohio and the Territory of Michigan to settle the matter. Both parties recruited motley armies to secure and hold the strip of land along the Maumee River; the land was desirable because it afforded a nice port on Lake Erie and the growing city of Toledo guarded a portion of a new canal between Erie and the Ohio River.

The armies never met on the battlefield –it seems to have been planned that way– and the casualties were limited to one wounded Michigan deputy sheriff (he recovered from a stab wound), two horses killed (or one mule, the records are unclear), and the loss of a few pigs and chickens to the foraging armies. In the end, Washington imposed a solution: Ohio was awarded the Toledo Strip and Michigan received statehood and, as a consolation prize, 16,347 square miles north of the Mackinac Straits.

Political solons and downstate newspapers cried a loud foul: Thanks, but no thanks, for "a region of perpetual snow, the Ultima Thule," said the *Detroit Free Press* in opposition to the compromise. A legislator was more graphic: "The Upper Peninsula," he stated, "is a sterile region on the shores of Lake Superior destined by soil and climate to remain forever a wilderness."

Times have changed, right? Wrong. Take a look at a map of Michigan. Notice that the Upper Peninsula is up, way up, north. About as far north as you can get. Then, observe that the region is almost surrounded by Lake Michigan, Lake Huron and the vast icy waters of Lake Superior.

Let's be honest here: The U.P. is a huge wasteland. You will find no palm trees, water parks or posh dude ranches up here in the frozen boonies.

There are lots of rivers up here. While they may seem ideally suited for canoeing and kayaking, keep in mind that the U.P. also has 140 waterfalls–not many visitors paddling happily down a wilderness river survive a plunge over Bond, Miners or Tahquamenon Falls.

What about fishing? You may have heard that the Upper Peninsula is an angler's paradise with the rivers and creeks just full of fish just waiting for your lure.

Not a good option: the rivers are very swift and cold; there are deep holes to swallow unsuspecting anglers and the waters are home to lethal creatures like snakes, snapping turtles and mermen. (The U.P. is so far north we don't even have mermaids. We have "mermen," part fish, part men–remnants of the last ice age.)

We do have lots of trees and rocks. The entire area is covered with deep, dark boreal forest; the woods are so huge and trackless that visitors wander off into the thickets and are never seen again. Since the U.P. is the southern portion of an ancient mountain range, we also have lots of rugged ankle-breaking granite everywhere.

Some folks make a sport of finding and climbing the highest point in all 50 states. Don't even think of trying to find Mt. Arvon which, at 1,979.238 feet, is listed as the highest point in Michigan. The route-finding directions to Mt. Arvon in the Baraga County Tourism and Recreation brochure will leave you reeling. Here's a small portion of the text:

> *The route on Ravine Road is as follows: At 0.7 miles, fork, go straight; 1.8 miles pass through gravel pit; 2.0 miles, leave gravel pit at a fork, go straight; 3.0 miles, fork, bear left; 3.4 miles, fork, bear right...*

And there are three more inches of single-spaced directions. Then, in a wonderfully-worded caveat, the reader is informed that "due to logging operations, the roads are often changed."

Anyway, not Mt. Arvon but a waste rock pile from open pit mining operations southeast of Negaunee is now actually the highest point in Michigan, and climbing even as we watch. Chambers of Commerce frown upon such revelations, so in the spirit of free inquiry I consider it my duty to pass it along to readers.

Take note, too, that there are more ghost towns in one Upper Peninsula county (Keweenaw) than in the entire Upper Midwest. What does that suggest to you? Yep, all the people who could get out got out long ago. And what did they leave behind? Ancient mine shafts filled with polluted water and thousands of disease-carrying bats, rusty nails, broken glass and discarded tin cans to cut your children's feet, and, most dangerous of all, descendants of long-ago miners who roam the dense forests and waste rock piles hoping to re-enact the movie *Deliverance* with innocent tourists,

All things considered, it's a mighty big risk to take a vacation—to say nothing of immigrating— to the Upper Peninsula. Doesn't it make sense to head for Florida, Texas or even Nebraska instead?

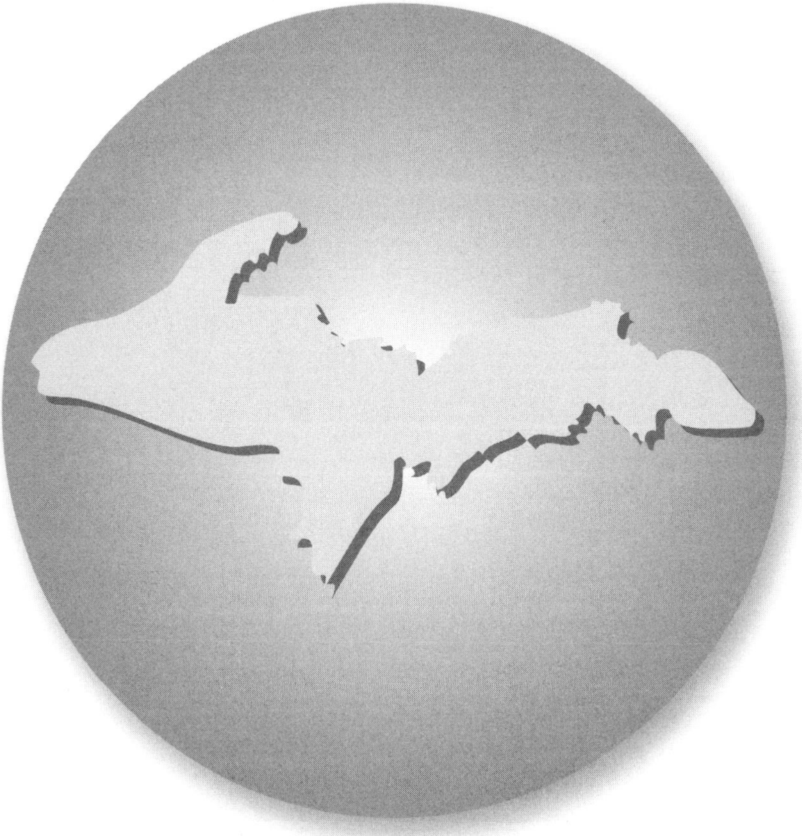

Climate

WE HAVE WEATHER IN THE UPPER PENINSULA. There is a distinct difference between climate and weather: Fresno, Tampa, Tucson, now those cities have a climate. The U.P. is a dark, frigid, snow-covered outpost where the Office of Homeland Security exiles various personalities until they show they can be allowed back into the United States.

The growing season up here is, according to the wishful thinkers in plant nurseries and tourist bureaus, a total of seventy-five frost-free days a year. All U.P. gardeners know you need to divide by two, maybe three, to get the real numbers.

The government has tried to keep it a secret, but long-time Yoopers know that the Upper Peninsula was selected by the

Donner Party to acclimatize themselves before they headed west to their fate in the snowy California mountains. They set up camp near Rockland in Ontonagon County, practiced winter survival skills and sorted through their collection of recipes.

The weather in the U.P. occurs in episodes, ranging from terrible to lethal. It can shift from one to the other in less than 15 minutes. There are only two seasons: a long glacial interlude and a very brief period of what we euphemistically call "summer." During this three-week second season, the local residents thaw out a bit, take their annual bath, entertain hordes of visitors and then get ready for winter. Think I exaggerate? There have been cases of hypothermia during the blueberry picking season. In August! A fashion note: It's really hard to pick blueberries wearing mittens.

Although we complain about the bad weather, we know that it keeps out the (ahem) riffraff. Nor do the hardy residents let snow, cold and rain keep them from taking part in outdoor activities. In fact, we are always amused (but secretly pleased) when a sprinkle of rain causes tourists to sprint for shelter. Maybe we are just stubborn or don't have a good grasp of the situation, but we refuse to cancel hikes or picnics because of impending storms.

My friend, Keith Dunstan, leads woods walks and bird watching outings; he always tells the participants up front about his stringent criteria for cancellation, I quote from Keith's directive:

> "There is a huge logging chain fastened to an oak tree in my backyard. When the wind is so strong it blows the chain out horizontal to the ground AND lightning is striking the chain links–then we stay home."

We even have our own winter cheerleader on a local television station.

Ray Bullock is an excitable-type weatherman and a storm freak. (He calls himself a meteorologist but, you know, in all the years I've watched him on TV he's never once talked about meteors. Go figure). He revels in massive snowfalls. When a winter storm hits the Upper Peninsula, Ray moves into the TV station with a sleeping bag and a cot and camps out so he won't miss a single flake of snow.

Whenever the annual snowfall reaches 300 inches–which happens most every year in these parts–he hosts a huge party; all the Yoopers celebrate by cutting a hole in the ice on Teal Lake in Negaunee and plunging into the frigid water. I've told you before that people are weird up here.

Speaking of weird, don't ever plan to visit the U.P. from February through April. The month of May, too, can be problematic. This is the time of the annual cabin fever pandemic. Beware! The disorder ranges from a fairly benign group that performs the Dance of the Wild

Cucumber on the frozen shoreline of Lake Superior. Every Thursday. In the nude. All the while chanting a little ditty over and over again: “Rocks and trees, snow and ice and seven degrees.” In its most severe form, cabin fever afflicts hunters and trappers who wander in the streets of small villages and discharge large caliber rifles at shadows and snowmobilers.

One winter, a Michigan State trooper newly transferred from a Detroit-area post to the U.P. was called to a domestic disturbance at a home on an island that shall remain nameless. When the trooper arrived, she found the man of the house cowering in a back bedroom, while his girlfriend and another woman chased each other around the living room with roaring chain saws. Once the situation was sorted out and the trooper returned to the Sault Ste. Marie post, she immediately applied for a transfer back to Detroit. Her parting words were, “I can deal with what happens in the cities, but I can't deal with cabin fever in the U.P."

Some Yoopers migrate to warmer climes each winter. They are shunned as cowards and weaklings. One senior citizen, Elmer Trebilcock, solved his winter problem without moving an inch. Elmer lives in a small bachelor cabin south of Iron River, Michigan, close to the border with Wisconsin. At least he thought he lived in Michigan until a Wisconsin State surveying team came through one year and informed him that his cabin was just over the state line. The following week a Wisconsin tax collector appeared and demanded payment on Elmer's delinquent property tax bill.

"What a relief," Elmer chortled to the tax collector, "Those Michigan winters were killing me."

michigan→
←Wisconsin

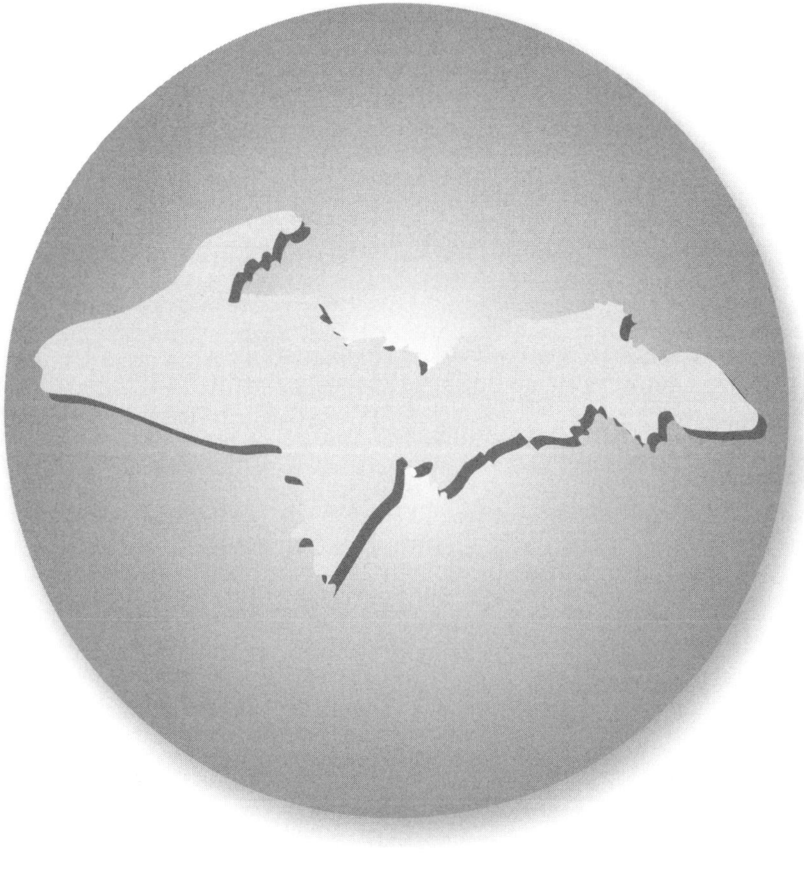

Insects

IT'S HARD TO BELIEVE, but despite the snow, intense cold and cabin fever, many U.P. residents prefer winter over the other seasons. The reason: When it warms up a bit, every biting insect known to entomologists emerges in dense clouds.

There are four particularly vicious bugs that wreak havoc and misery on humans from late May to September.

First out of the swamps is the *blackfly*, a small pesky critter that dines on insect repellent. Most local residents are not particularly upset even by swarms of the little buggers. Most of us, as a matter of fact, are immune to blackfly attacks after years of enduring multiple bites. The hard layer of permafrost just under the skin of Yoopers also helps to deflect the nasty insects. Besides, some women who live up here go out into wet areas purposely each spring to get bitten; the toxin injected by blackflies puffs up one's face and eliminates wrinkles. It's less expensive than Botox or cosmetic surgery.

When Fred Rule leads wildflower walks in May and June, he seems to delight in frequenting the most likely areas to encounter blackflies. Immune to their bites after decades of exposure, Fred will stop in a wet thicket and launch into a lengthy rambling anecdote. If he notes that the participants are swatting flies, he extends his story to a lecture about the several distinct species of blackflies.

"Some species are extinct," he informs the group of squirming downstate visitors, and after a long pause he adds, "We don't have those kind here." No one appreciates Fred's attempt at levity.

If Fred is feeling particularly feisty, he will observe laconically that it's a good thing the blackflies are not biting this morning. And besides, he points out, blackflies–at least the males–help to pollinate the blueberry blossoms.

Even fifth-generation Yoopers like me despise *wood ticks*. They are the worst of the worst. A widely-known and well-respected gastroenterologist has a sign on his office desk proclaiming, "I HATE TICKS!"

What most patients don't realize is that the sign has a double meaning. When Dr. Nicholls reviewed a routine colonoscopy screening for a middle-aged female patient recently, he pointed out that she had a number of small pouches (diverticula), but that this was common in older people. As he usually did, the physician use the abbreviation "tics" to refer to the pouches in her colon. When the patient became agitated and asked how on earth ticks could have gotten into her intestine, Dr. Nicholl's puckish sense of humor took over and he responded gravely, "Well, if you were having a picnic and sat on the grass...."

These little eight-legged blood suckers are stealthy: They jump on your clothing, hide out for a while and then slowly, carefully they crawl under your shirt or pants to find a warm, secluded spot to tap your body fluids. Invariably they aim for your private parts. It makes people do crazy things:

Frank Tregumbo and Dick Rowse were playing their usual Thursday morning game of golf at the Gray Wolf Links. Frank, as he commonly does, was carrying on a running monologue–reviewing his accomplishments, his prowess with women and so forth. Every time he made a good golf shot, Frank proclaimed loudly, "Fan-damn-tastic!" Dick was not amused. He had heard all of Frank's balderdash before and he was irritated more than usual because he had run into a swarm of wood ticks on the Bay de Noc-Grand Island hiking trail. One tick had burrowed itself into a very private part of his anatomy, producing severe swelling, and he was in misery.

Finally, on the 10th tee, Frank hit a stupendous drive, more than 200 yards and straight down the fairway. “FAN-DAMN-TASTIC!” Frank roared and did a Cornish jig, pretending his driver was a dance partner. Dick went bonkers. Quickly, he unbuckled his pants and pulled down his boxer shorts. He pointed to his swollen and previously private parts and bellered, WOOD-DAMN-TICK!”

How do you get rid of a tick that has tunneled into your skin? Most people are so appalled to find the hard-shelled bug on them, they rip it off in a frenzy. Alas, that leaves the tick’s mouth parts embedded in your flesh; this can lead to terrible infections. Glen Trezona, one of my neighbors, has a strange sense of humor (some unkind folks say he’s not quite right in the head). After a particularly tick-infested hike with a group of friends, he made small wooden lapel pins for each hiker. The pins featured real wood ticks–encased in spar varnish–and cryptic (pun intended) inscriptions that bemused even Yoopers: "Ticks forever," "Pet ticks" or "Fantasticks." Wood ticks are incredibly difficult to kill. Just this past summer one of the little buggers went through an entire wash cycle. When my wife pulled a shirt out of the machine to put it in the dryer, the tick waltzed away!

People who read the first edition of this book, *You Wouldn't Like It Here*, scoffed at the story about U.P. *mosquitoes* mating with turkeys. An example of Yooper exaggeration, they said. Actually, they were right about the mosquito-turkey affair. The source for the sighting of the mosquito-turkey love making, Dean Trenary, revealed that he didn't think what he and his buddies had really seen would ever be believed. So he downsized his tale a bit to maintain his credibility.

In point of fact, a bunch of the good old boys from Limestone saw it happen on the west side of the AuTrain Basin: A male mosquito was actually trying to mate with a Sandhill Crane. One of the guys had a digital camera and tried to get a photograph of the act, but the sun was going down and there was not enough light. At least they thought it was a crane but it could have been a Great Blue Heron. Anyway it was a huge bird, way bigger than a hen turkey. At any rate, it is no exaggeration that there are thousands of mosquitoes in the Upper Peninsula, especially after a heavy snow year. Which pretty much describes every year here in the north.

Visitors complain that mosquitoes target them much more than the local residents. That probably is true. Families in Covington, McFarland and Brevort have trained their mosquitoes to swarm and attack when they see designer clothing or out-of-state license plates.

The good news is that the whiny blood-suckers do not carry the West Nile Virus.

XO

Even better news is that they do carry an East Nile Virus. Instead of debilitating the individual, it acts as an aphrodisiac. With Yooper men such a diffident and sluggish lot, an annual shot of East Nile Virus is the only thing that keeps the birthrate stable.

Deer flies are the friends of law enforcement personnel in the Upper Peninsula. If wood ticks are the insect form of stealth bombers, then deer flies are Hell Cat fighter planes. They announce their arrival loudly and will not abandon an attack until they make a hole in your skin. When inmates escape from our local prisons, they usually flee to the deep woods to hide. But in a very short time they realize that they have made a big mistake. Exhausted, covered with bug bites and almost hysterical, the cons pound on the prison gates and plead to be put back in their cells.

All the tourist-tempting brochures advise–in very small print–that visitors should bring a supply of insect repellent when they come to the Upper Peninsula. What they don't say is most bug dope is not that effective against our industrial strength insects. And that those that are strong enough to really work spill toxic ingredients into your blood stream.

A climate-controlled spa in Traverse City would be a much better destination for a vacation. Don't you agree?

Wildlife

THE TOURIST INDUSTRY WANTS YOU–and your money–and they have no shame. They spin tales about the abundant wildlife in the Upper Peninsula. They try to lure people up here by promising views of graceful deer, friendly bears and other cuddly wild animals. And the visitors come, enticed by a Disney notion of wildlife–come see Bambi and Smokey Bear scamper out of the forest and eat from your hand. More likely, they will bite the hand that feeds them. In the interest of full disclosure, here's the real deal about our wild critters.

There are almost a half-million *whitetail deer* roaming the vast forests of the U.P. That's a deer-and-a-half for every man, woman and child living up here. What the slick brochures don't tell you is that the deer have become furry terrorists, committed to destroying or damaging your Jeep or Trail Blazer. Do you know why they are doing this? Because they have lost so many of their relatives to vehicles and hunters over the years and they are out for revenge on your SUV.

Sure, you can watch the road ahead, at least during daylight hours, but the U.P. deer have become very sophisticated in their mission: They have learned to run out of the woods and crash into the *side* of your vehicle. Good luck getting an insurance adjuster to take your claim; they are out trapping timber wolves in Minnesota. The insurance industry wants to bring the wolves back to kill off the deer–they know what the expensive bottom line is when it comes to car/deer accidents.

If you do manage to track down an insurance agent, he will be surly and doubtful; he will demand a pound of raw venison as proof of your claim. You and your vehicle will not be in sympathetic hands in the Upper Peninsula.

Many of the car-deer accidents occur during the fall. This is the time of the annual mating season and deer are more active. Remember too, there are hundreds of lusty deer hunters roaming the woods at the same time, if you take my meaning.

There are 20,000 *black bears* in the woods of the U.P., according to current estimates, and they are perpetually hungry. The furry beasts like to mug hikers for the food in their packs; they are constantly breaking into cottages and consider dogs and cats as attractive snacks. Black bears have very sensitive noses; last summer a large sow bear broke into a new silver Lincoln Town car parked at a trailhead to retrieve a package of Life Savers left in the glove box.

If you choose to ignore my warnings about bears and come up here to walk in the woods, be prepared. But not too prepared. Keep in mind what happened to one chap from Grosse Pointe a couple of years ago:

BEAR
Lake of
the Clouds

Although deathly afraid of bears, George Vivian wanted to hike in the Porcupine Mountain Wilderness State Park. A friend advised him to buy some bear pepper spray as a deterrent. George motored to the western Upper Peninsula, emerged from his Ford Expedition, donned a new pack, proceeded to spray himself from head to toe with the pepper spray and collapsed in shock!

Fortunately a passerby observed the action and summoned an ambulance. Later, in his hospital bed, George was asked why he had drenched himself in spray. Through coughs and wheezes, he explained that he thought pepper spray was like insect repellent and he needed to douse himself to keep bears away.

The *wolf* population is on the rise in the Upper Peninsula. So, if by some remote chance you do come to the U.P., don't wear anything red–not even a thong–because the wolves have been reading about the little girl from the 'hood.

The Michigan Department of Natural Resources insists that there are no *mountain lions* living in the Upper Peninsula. Residents insist that there are–and that they have seen them. Should you encounter one here in the dense forests, both you and the lion have misinterpreted the facts. While you are immobilized in panic, the lion is debating: Are you going to be his dinner?

At any rate, don't expect help from any governmental agency. The mountain lion doesn't exist.

With all the wilderness up here, it is great habitat for birds of prey. *Owls* take great pleasure in bedeviling tourists and newcomers by roosting in trees outside their rental cabin and hooting throughout the night. Do you want a Yooper barred owl to call (and call, and call) your name at 2 am? "Whoooo cooks for you? Whooo cooks for you-all?" Owls also go after pets. Just the other day a Great Horned Owl carried off a miniature poodle named Mergatroid at a park in downtown Bergland.

There are plenty of other wild animals living up here in the boonies, and they are just as mean and surly as the human residents. *Porcupines* love to chew on your tires and radiator hoses. *Raccoons* dump over garbage cans and take bites out of your children. *Skunks* offer a lingering cologne-au-Yooper almost everywhere.

Now you know how civilized our wild region is. You will have a much better vacation at the Grand Canyon or the Everglades.

THE Local RESIDENTS

HAVE YOU BEEN PAYING ATTENTION? Now, really, can't you see why you wouldn't like it here—not for a visit or, most certainly, not as a place to call home. Those who do live here know that the Upper Peninsula is a dismal region of forbiddingly frigid weather, dark gloomy forests, hordes of biting insects, dangerous wild animals and somewhat quirky human residents.

Oh, sure, on first impression during your brief vacation the land may seem like a paradise, the perfect respite from your city life, and we may seem normal, even a bit friendly. But we have our own brand of misery from being cold and isolated too long. Don't expect us to give you welcoming bouquets or, despite what you may have heard, sing quaint shanty songs for your amusement.

Residents are suspicious of strangers. If you get the feeling you are being watched from behind rocks and trees—and you probably are—locate an escape route immediately. When entering a restaurant, select a table so you can sit with your back to a wall. Try not to make eye contact with any of the locals, even the servers. Don't drink the water or order anything called "garbage omelet" or "lumberjack stew." It is usually wise not to order the special of the day either—just in case it could be be the remains of animals scraped off the highway.

Keep in mind that we live here in the wilds far away from any organized law enforcement and we don't follow the usual norms of human interaction. So, don't get too friendly or trusting. Everyone up here seems normal until you get to know them.

The quirks emerge in full blown adolescent humor, especially when we are forced to go "down below." Even persons with college degrees and responsible jobs have difficulty controlling their inner adolescent:

> The Dismal Seepage Community School District sent Ron Tresedder down to the lower Peninsula one summer to update his teaching credentials. Ron had been assigned to teach a new course on human reproduction for high school students in the fall.
>
> Held at Michigan State University, the summer workshop was taught by Dr. Harold Gordon, physiologist and expert on the topic of sex education. Perhaps to emphasize his expertise, Dr. Gordon always wore a long white lab coat, unbuttoned, over his street clothes.
>
> On the first day of class, Dr. Gordon strode purposefully into the lecture hall holding aloft a clear glass bottle with an object immersed in liquid. Walking close

> to the front row of students he held the specimen even higher.
>
> Ron noted that the professor's left hand was in the pocket of his trousers. Clearing his throat for attention, Dr. Gordon pronounced "In my hand I hold a diseased penis." The class was momentarily transfixed until Ron, unable to inhibit his inner adolescent, called out from his seat in the back row, "What ya got in the bottle, Doc?"

You might expect that aging would mellow the whimsical behavior of our regional residents. Not so:

> Walter Couch, a lonely widower for several years, decided on his 90th birthday to seek some female companionship. Dressing himself carefully in his best flannel shirt and Carhartt work pants, he sprinkled himself with cologne and headed out to the Michigan House Bistro and Pub. Spying an elderly woman sitting at the bar,

> he sauntered over, took the stool beside her and ordered a drink. Trying to look very cool, Walter took a sip of his drink, turned to the lady and asked, "So, can you tell me, do I come here often?"

Most Yooper men don't talk much except with their hunting and drinking buddies. They are especially quiet around outsiders. We came up here many years ago when no one else wanted the region and created a way of life that involves hunting and gathering, outhouses and prolonged suffering. We like it just the way it is.

Yoopers resent any interference or restrictions to their life style. We know that visitors see us as a primitive life form. Why else would we live in a cold and remote environ, is the message that comes through loud and clear. We can read between the lines: If we were talented or capable we would be living a life of ease and affluence in some more populated venue. Yoopers get a lot of of patronizing advice from outsiders:

> Johnny Kitto was sitting outside a country store in Watersmeet happily working his way through a pile of candy bars when a tourist stopped and admonished the 12-year-old boy.
>
> "Don't you know that all that sugar and fat is not good for you?" he asked rhetorically.
>
> Johnny looked up and responded with what seemed like a non sequitur: "My grandpa Kitto lived to be 97."
>
> "Well, did he eat lots of candy bars?" the bewildered troll asked.
>
> "Nope. He minded his own business," said Johnny unwrapping another Snickers bar.

Tony Nancarrow owns a popular *pasty** shop in Laurium. Over more than two

*A *pasty* (pronounced pass-tee if you want to sound like a native) is a meal in a crust that was brought to the Upper Peninsula by Cornish immigrants. It's probably best not to ask about the specific ingredients or, even in a joking way, suggest the baker might have used ingredients found near roadways in preparing the U.P. staple.

decades he has kept track of how many times (5,433) visitors have pranced into his shop and demanded: "Don't you know how to spell *pastry*?" Tony has learned to immobilize his interrogators with the Upper Peninsula stare. This is not a mere glance of disapproval. The U.P. stare usually lasts longer than a minute and can produce serious side effects for the recipient. It creates a frigid silence that pummels the visitor like a November gale on Lake Superior. The icy psychic withdrawal withers anyone in its path.

So, beware: If you ask a Yooper where you might bag a trophy whitetail deer, find a good raspberry picking spot or what he thinks about the movie *Escanaba In Da Moonlight*, you are sure to get the U.P. stare. And you won't thaw out until you head south.

One other thing: Don't tell Yoopers to have a nice day. They know what kind of miserable day they are bound to have, the same they have endured all their lives. Cheery advice to experience anything "nice" in the U.P, just rubs salt in ancient wounds.

Yooper Talk

Don't be alarmed by lack of eye contact and sluggish verbal responses during those times–medical emergencies, seeking directions, finding Uncle Milton who has wandered off into the woods–when it is absolutely necessary to communicate with the residents.

Unless you know the International Phonetic Alphabet or are an expert dialectician and grammarian, you probably won't understand what a Yooper is saying anyway. The residents of this remote outpost have a very distinct speech pattern. Linguists maintain there is nothing similar in the Upper Midwest, indeed in the entire North American continent.

Many years ago a very diverse group of immigrants drifted into the Upper Peninsula to mine copper and iron, harvest the vast stands of white pine trees and seek refuge from law enforcement authorities. There were Cornish, Italians,

Finns, Germans, French and at least a score of other ethnic groups represented. So, here's how it happened that a distinctive and unintelligible form of speaking arose:

-Put all those different languages in a verbal blender and run it on high for many years.

-Isolate the polyglot speakers for a century and a half.

-Add in the impact of inbreeding, cold weather (it inhibits easy movements of lips and tongue) and a vocabulary limited to fifty words.

Behold! You have Yooper talk.

The first thing visitors notice is the U.P. melody pattern, where phrases veer up, around and down in exotic rhythms. Confusing the listener even more is the random omission and substitution of speech sounds. Do you know what this Yooper of Cornish heritage is saying?

"Feed ta 'orse some hoats and 'ay."

or

"Look at those bloody hants going hup and down tha' 'emlock tree."

What about this example that stems from Finnish and German influence:

"Dis, dat and the udder ting."

Then, contributed by French Canadians, a startling little cry of "eh" or "hey" added to all declarative statements:

"How about them Packers, eh?"

You will sense that a Yooper is speaking English but in some strange form. Don't agree to anything a local says unless you have it in writing. Be especially vigilant if, in some moment of weakness, you ask for directions from a resident.

You Can Miss It

Visitors to the Upper Peninsula should keep in mind that getting people lost is one of the few pleasures we have in this frozen wasteland. Old Eddie Uren is a legend and grand poohbah at getting tourists lost in the vast forests. Last fall, at a coffee shop in Manistique, two mushroom seekers from Grand Rapids made the mistake of asking Eddie where they might find morels in the Hiawatha National Forest. I scribbled down on a napkin exactly what Eddie told them:

> Head northwest on County Road 442. After two miles or thereabouts, it will turn to gravel. Proceed on for several miles–I'd say about 6.2 miles–and look for a blighted elm tree in an old farm field; it's easy to spot because a Holstein cow with three black spots on its right side will be grazing there.
>
> Turn right on the next two-track road and go exactly 54 rods through the woods to Whiskey Creek. Park by a dead popple tree with a blue jay's nest in the third crotch on the north side..."

At this point the tourists' eyes were glazing over and they made furtive movements of distress. Backing slowly away, they offered thanks and then fled toward the front door.

> "There's an old broken down outhouse on the edge of the field," Old Eddie called out and then, sporting an angelic smile added, "You can miss it."

As the confused trolls ran to their car, the coffee shop patrons gave Eddie a standing ovation.

Why are visitors so fascinated and amused by the fact that some of us still have outhouses? And why is it that the most frequently asked question at Upper Peninsula parks is "Where's the rest room?"

Yes, visitors, there are outhouses in the U.P. By all means ask about them because we are amused by your pottyphilia and have lots of bathroom humor we just love to share.

Now, although it's possible that I have been exaggerating a trifle earlier in this guide, the following outhouse tale is absolutely true. I have sworn affidavits from five individuals who were present to see this event unfold:

> Dale Chenoweth volunteered to lead several summer hikes for a regional Life Long Learning Association.
>
> The first outing was a walk to see Chapel Falls, in the Pictured' Rocks National Lakeshore. Ten hikers met Dale at the Chapel Trailhead on a glorious summer morning.
>
> As the group fiddled with their daypacks, Dale advised everyone to use the nearby outhouse before starting the hike; it was the last toilet they would find on the trail.
>
> Shortly after Melissa Lutey entered the bathroom, the assembled group–and not a few tourists–heard her shriek and then start crying. Rushing to her aid,

two female hikers discovered that, somehow, Melissa had dropped a brand-new pair of expensive binoculars down the toilet hole. It nestled precariously in among all sorts of unspeakable material.

"Leave it!" commanded Dale, not wanting to even think about the process of retrieving the optics.

"But," Melissa wailed, "It's a birthday gift from my daughters!"

An elderly gentleman, president of the Life Long Learning Association, offered to help and hurried to his truck. When he returned with a fishing pole, complete with monofilament line and a dangling Swedish Pimple lure, Dale threw up his hands in disgust and stalked away in high dudgeon.

For the next 30 minutes a team of five participants took brief turns–the odors emanating from the toilet were enough to damage

LAST →
CHANCE
CHAPEL
← FALLS

delicate nasal membranes–trying to extricate the binoculars with hook and line.

This trail head parking lot of the Pictured Rocks National Lakeshore is heavily visited and several groups of tourists arrived and prepared to walk to the falls and Lake Superior beach.

When they saw the inexplicable activity of several people "fishing" in a toilet, many visitors, remembering the warnings about Yooper eccentricities, got back in their vehicles and zoomed off.

The tale ends with good news and bad news. They did manage to "fish" out the binoculars. And Melissa carried the optics all the way to the falls and washed them off. The bad news is that she was cited by a park ranger for fishing without a license.

Bringing Culture to the U.P.

Residents take immense pleasure in playing with tourists' heads, particularly fussy or self-important visitors who are bent on impressing us with their refinement and sense of culture. So, by all means act superior when you talk with local residents. We welcome the challenge.

One morning in May last year, Bob Trembath and I were having coffee and a peach scone in the Rolling Stone Café in the Western Upper Peninsula before going sauntering in the woods to look for wildflowers.

We were nicely tucked into the tasty scones when a middle-aged man made a flamboyant entrance into the Café. Pausing just inside the front door, he seemed to preen and posture as if waiting for a drum roll and a round of applause. Man, did he look out of place.

His suit coat was draped over his shoulders like a cape and he carried a short black walking stick with an ivory handle. He twirled the stick in dramatic flourish and stepped up to the cash register where Julia, the owner of the Rolling Stone Café, was making change for a customer.

"My name is Dr. J. Barksdale Glenn," he intoned in a affected, dramatic voice, "Professor emeritus at the University of Michigan. I am the creator of the first mobile art display in the Midwest." Julia stopped in mid-task and stared in open-mouthed amazement at Dr. J. Barksdale Glenn, professor emeritus of the University of Michigan.

"I'm seeking suitable sites for my mobile art display," Professor emeritus Glenn continued and then, smirking broadly, added, "And sampling the local culture." Glenn actually glowed with the self-satisfied demeanor of a man who takes daily pleasure reflecting on the happy fact that he is Professor emeritus J. Barksdale Glenn, creator of the first mobile art display in the Midwest.

I just knew what Julia would do next and

winced at the prospect of dealing with J. Barksdale Glenn.

"Why don't you talk to those guys at the round table back there; they are long-time residents and regulars at the Café," Julia said, pointing at Bob and me. Bob winked at me and whispered something about "here comes some fun."

Dr. Glenn approached our table with a princely swagger. "My name is Dr. J. Barksdale Glenn," he announced, "Professor emeritus at the University of Michigan. I created the first mobile art display in the Midwest."

We just looked at him.

"Are you gentlemen old timers in this area?" Dr, Glenn asked while taking a seat at our table, "And, by the way, what does one do up here to enrich one's mind?"

We just gave him our best U.P. stare. Seemingly unaffected by the cold silence, Glenn continued: "But, ah yes, is it not true that the Upper Peninsula is like a cup of yogurt: No active culture?"

Professor Glenn paused and laughed, really a dry chuckle. It sounded to me like a chipmunk with a chronic gastrointestinal problem.

"What say, gentlemen?" Glenn challenged.

When Bob and I sat mutely contemplating the Professor emeritus apparition, Dr. Glenn launched into a lengthy monologue about his efforts to promote the fine arts. Pretending he was taking notes, Bob Trembath slipped me a missive evaluating Glenn's monologue: "A series of pretty phrases marching over a hill in search of an idea." I knew then that the Professor emeritus had unwittingly walked into Bob's trap. Things were going to get very interesting.

When Glenn paused for a moment. Bob, doing a pretty good impression of Columbo, the seemingly bewildered detective on a television series, interrupted.

"Dr. Glenn, we have a story up here that none of us can really understand. So, Doctor, maybe you can help interpret its meaning. Let me tell you the tale, Doctor, and I'm sure you can help us." I took a sip of Grand Island Roast coffee and sat back to enjoy the show as Bob began to spin one of his famous shaggy dog stories:

> "This tale takes place in equatorial Africa, Two hippos are lounging in a fetid pool of water in the deep, steamy jungle. Slime covers the surface of the water and hordes of insects hover around the hippos' eyes and noses. To escape the heat, the hippos have been standing in the shallow water for several days, not moving, not even to forage. They have barely acknowledged each other all this time.
>
> Finally, one hippo rouses himself and says to his companion, 'I can't believe it's Thursday.'"

Dr. J. Barksdale Glenn sat stunned when Bob concluded his tale, his right eyelid twitching uncontrollably. Bob leaned in closer to Glenn and asked, "Doc, your name, what's the J. stand for?"

"Um, well, J-J-John," the professor responded.

"Well now, Johnny," Bob said, "I will understand if you, being from the Lower Peninsula, can't explain the lesson of the story, but here's a hint: Think of the word, 'ultra-crepifarian' and then you can figure it out."

Professor emeritus Glenn closed his eyes a moment and then, without a word, stood up abruptly and headed for the men's room. After watching his unceremonious retreat, I looked back at our table just in time to stop my unpredictable friend Bob Trembath from placing a small fingernail paring in the Professor's breakfast quiche.

The spring wildflowers were particularly stunning that morning.

U.P. Women

The women in the Upper Peninsula are desperate for attention, to say nothing about a little affection. The men up here believe it "spoils" a woman to give her a compliment or tell her that he loves her. When confronted about this, Yooper men counter with something like this: "Hey, I told my wife I loved her when we got married–why should I have to say it again unless I change my mind?"

Although Alfred Penver's wife is an excellent cook, he never says *anything* appreciative about her culinary skills. When Eliza asks Al if he likes her pot roast or apple pie, he just grunts, "I'm eating it, ain't I?"

Some women get so fed up with their lethargic mates that they seek professional intervention. After 41 years of marriage to phlegmatic and indifferent Dennis, Helen Pendray had all she could take. She nagged Dennis for three weeks before he reluctantly agreed to attend counseling sessions together.

Since she was the complainant, the counselor asked Helen to speak first and share her frustration and pain. In excruciating detail, Helen described how Dennis took her for granted, gave her little or no attention and never expressed any affection.

"All he does is putter around in his workshop, roam the woods or bullshit with his cronies. And even when he's in the house, he's either watching TV or playing solitaire."

Finally, the counselor stood up and said, "O.K., Helen, I get the picture. I don't need to hear from Dennis. I know exactly what you need."

Walking over to where Helen sat crying softly, the counselor lifted her to her feet, wrapped her in a full frontal embrace and gave her a long passionate kiss. Turning to Dennis, who during the entire session had been mining for wax in his ear canals, the counselor asked, "Now, Dennis, that is exactly what your wife needs at least three times a week. Can you see that she gets it?"

Rousing himself from his chronic taciturn torpor, Dennis replied, "Well, Doc, I'm kinda busy... I can only bring her in here once a week."

Some Upper Peninsula wives turn despair into a competitive game. It's called "Last Woman Standing" and here is how it is played:

> The playing field is a dinner table where a sizable number of

relatives or other guests are present. A small tag team of women who did all the preparations for the meal wait until all the other diners are seated. Then the team sits down but all remain poised, on the edge of their chairs.

One woman announces that she forgot the gravy, bustles about bringing a gravy boat to the table and then takes her chair.

Almost immediately another team member jumps up and explains she has to check the pies in the oven. All the guests sit stiffly with forks and knives poised.

That is when the men, anxious to eat and impatient with the delay, go into action, "Gertrude, sit down now so we can begin." "Lucille, you're rocking the boat, sit down."

These ejaculations reach a crescendo with a resounding "SIT DOWN!" The last woman

S
P

standing when the husbands approach terminal impatience is the winner.

Yooper Health Care

If you choose to visit the Upper Peninsula, you must be alert every minute. Don't try to buy gas, order a meal, get in an accident or find a motel room on November 15, or the last Saturday in April. These are High Holy Days–the opening of the deer hunting season and the start of the trout fishing season–and are U.P. National Holidays. It's rumored that even the hospitals close their doors.

Yoopers are so perverse they find humor in serious issues like health care and hospitals. There was a widely circulated rumor last year that many old gents residing in the regional nursing homes were getting large doses of *Viagra*®. When asked about the rumor, the director of the Pine Stump Junction Rest Home did acknowledge massive purchases of the little blue pill. Somewhat cryptically, he added that, since the purchase of the medication, there had not been a single instance of an elderly male resident rolling out of bed at night.

"It's easier than erecting barriers on the sides of every bed," the director concluded with just the hint of a smile.

Ben Pollack had pondered the persistent philosophical question about the equality of all men for many years. When he contracted bladder cancer, Ben was scheduled for quarterly checkups at a regional medical center. (I'll leave it to your imagination by what route the bladder is accessed with a scope on the end of a long thin tube.) After two years of the somewhat embarrassing procedures, he summoned up the courage to ask a friendly nurse for her opinion on his persistent question.

Without even looking up from her duties of preparing Ben, Lydia stated, "After almost two decades of nursing and assisting in dozens of these cystoscopic procedures, I can answer unequivocally: *"All men are <u>not</u> created equal!"*

It is well-known that mistakes, some with tragic outcomes, can and do occur in hospitals. A breakdown in communication created an upheaval of epic proportions at a Copper Country hospital.

While parking his car one morning in August, a resident physician noticed a shiny new foreign automobile with its lights blinking. Stopping at the main reception desk, he wrote a note–in his best physician scribble–for the public address assistant. Imagine his amused surprise, to say nothing about a collective and very audible cheer from the staff and patients, when the announcement was read. Unable to decipher the penmanship of the hurrying doctor, the inexperienced public address worker interpreted the message thusly;

> "There is a red vulva, with its lights blinking, in the east parking lot."

Two male orderlies and an intern rushed down the stairs and into the parking lot to check out the action.

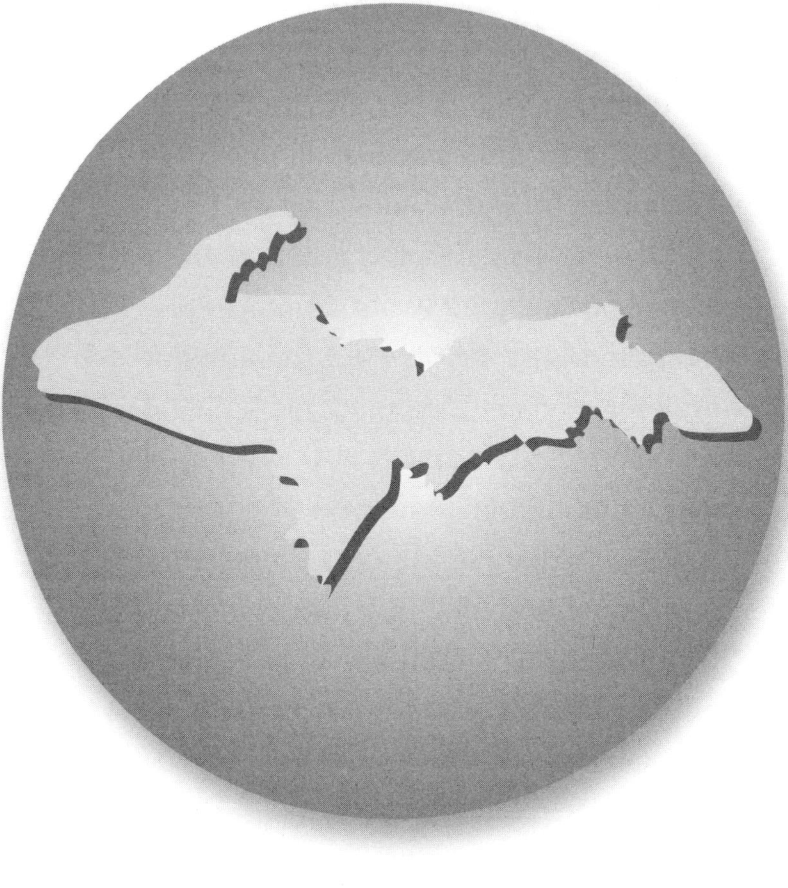

FINDING A Place TO STAY

Most people who have been to the Upper Peninsula would advise you not to stay overnight. Keep on going west to, say, the Mayo Clinic and have a colonoscopy, or even further, to Iowa, and take a tour of the pig farms. Anything is better than trying to find a place to stay up here. Yes, you could stay in chain motels alongside the "highways" (read: two-lane roads), places so much like those in Sioux Falls or San Luis Obispo that you won't even know you are in the Upper Peninsula at all. But no, you promised your family that this time you would find the real U.P., you would experience the local ambiance and backwoods charm. Ignore my advice and here is what you are likely to find:

A run down resort named Sea Gull Harbor located on a chilly and desolate rocky shore of Lake Superior. The granite is abrasive and uncomfortable to sit on and the lake water is only 59 degrees even in "summer."

Sea Gull Harbor is so far off the electric grid that power is supplied by an ancient generator; when it revs up, which is almost all the time, it sounds like the entire Israeli Army tank corps at full-throttle. The generator runs from six in the morning to ten in the evening. You will need to bring ear plugs.

The resort is run by Earl and Ellen Pendarvis. Ellen inherited the business from her father who founded Sea Gull Harbor in 1927. Nothing much has changed since then.

In order to cut overhead, Ellen and Earl have eliminated unimportant things in the rustic cabins–things like maintenance, heat, running water and indoor bathrooms.

Ellen does all the labor of running the the resort and shows grave physical evidence of deficit living. She complains loudly and at length to any guest who will listen about her bunions and hemorrhoids (don't be off-put by the tube of Preparation H she wears on a string around her neck–she usually washes her hands before changing the pillow cases).

Earl, on the other hand, fancies himself the impresario of Sea Gull Harbor. He spends his days ambling about the resort with his old dog, Piran, a black Lab that emits waves of terrible odor. Earl and Piran may appear at your cabin before six in the morning to deliver a weather report and then honor you with lengthy stories that have many digressions and no discernable point.

When you arrive at the resort, another tourist who is checking out will be trying to convince Ellen he should get a discount because a regiment of ants was also living in his cabin. Ellen will put this uppity troll in his place by snapping, "Hey dude, you said you wanted rustic!"

Since the Sea Gull Harbor resort is at least 37 miles from a restaurant, Ellen and Earl offer short order meals in a tiny grill

Office

that originally served Ernest Hemingway and Al Capone when they fished the Two-Hearted River. The entire kitchen area is covered with at least four inches of pre-Cambrian grease. The two cook/servers, Hilka and Elvira, scrape off a layer each week for the deep-fry unit.

The menu is very limited. They offer no breakfast; Earl makes jokes about combing the shoreline to find seaweed or other flotsam. Lunch consists of either tuna or egg salad sandwiches, stale potato chips and a sprig of wintergreen to prevent scurvy. For dinner, there is only one entree: Pasties.

In case you are interested, here is the weekly dinner menu:

Monday:	pork and potato pasty
Tuesday:	beef and rutabaga pasty
Wednesday:	Don't ask and don't tell pasty
Thursday:	kidney pasty
Friday:	carp pasty
Saturday:	combination pasty (all of the above)
Sunday:	a day of fasting

Don't try to get to know Hilka and Elvira or, at the risk of finding new, unwelcome ingredients in your pasty, ask for any special treatment. The two cooks are older than diorite and have heard it all before; their husbands left them for younger women, nubile sisters from Chicago, and the only outlet they have for pent up resentment is to punish the customers.

Then, the final straw, shortly after the generator is turned off, and you start to enjoy the blessed quiet and the sound of the waves on Lake Superior, a trio of love-sick whip-poor-wills will arrive and chant their dreary mantra all night just outside your vintage cabin.

Don't risk it–keep on driving.

Entertainment

SO, DURING YOUR FAMILY TRIP to the Upper Peninsula, you are hoping to find entertainment to keep the kids from whining and your in-laws from discussing your faults. Don't even consider coming up here looking for fun. Instead, attend the annual stamp collectors' convention in Peoria or audition for a reality television show featuring competitive eating. But, since you may already be here, let's review what dire options await you.

There are, at last counting, 33 *museums* in the U.P.–if you include the two that display the names and photographs of visitors who were eaten by bears, disappeared in the woods, or thought they could eat two pasties in one sitting. All the museums are located in abandoned mine shafts, rickety old ore boats or decrepit buildings formerly used to house CCC men in the 1930s. The elderly men and women who staff the museums have had to agree that they, too, would be on display as living history.

Although I would strongly advise against it, you could attend one of our quaint local festivals:

-The annual winter outhouse race. Teams of slightly demented, tipsy participants push decorated outdoor potties down through the icy streets of a small town. After the race, visit the Outhouse Hall of Fame.

-The annual haircut watching fair. Teams of slightly disturbed, sleepy participants spend an entire day watching patrons receive haircuts in overheated barbershops. Don't miss the U.P. Barbers and Cosmetologists Hall of Fame.

-The annual pasty throwing contest. Teams of slightly unstable, overfed participants gather at Lake Independence and compete to see who can chuck a pasty the furthest. Coming soon, the newest theme park: Pasty World.

The more active tourist may be looking forward to such opportunities as:

Water sports. One of the tricks which entices people to the visit the U.P. is the promotion of water sports–swimming, kayaking, canoeing, fishing, and boating. And it does look like great family fun.

Not mentioned is that for most of the year the lakes and rivers are covered with ice and snow. Truth in advertising compels me to add that the survival time for immersion in any water up here is measured in seconds. And all year round our waters are home to dangerous creatures like polar bears, elephant seals, packs of wolves and, some say, sea monsters in the deepest waters.

Hiking. No one hikes in the U.P. Take your cue from the locals–they don't hike just for the sake of hiking, even through beautiful woods and by rocky shorelines. They scurry from spot to spot to get out of the cold, avoid the bugs and escape other Yoopers hiding out in those woods, playing banjos and pretending to re-enact scary movies.

Camping. Come on now, let's be honest. The people who live up here know that simply living in the Upper Peninsula is camping. Why would they want to go further into the woods?

There are some seedy taverns you might visit. In most every case, the bars up here are overheated, dimly-lit and smell of stale beer and other odors wafting from the back room. The bartender will be a tall, thin character named Leon with long, grimy hair and a tattoo on his right bicep proclaiming "Death before Dishonor." On the wall behind the bar is a large mural depicting Custer's Last Stand and a bumper sticker proclaiming *To take away my deer rifle, you will have to pry it from my cold, dead hands.*

A trio of beefy locals with substantial beer bellies will be perched on stools at the bar. They will be muttering darkly about the Dee-En-Are (Michigan Department of Natural Resources), United Nations Black Helicopters and timber wolves killing all their deer. Because their jeans are buckled so low on their ample hips, when they lean forward to put out a cigarette or fill up a glass, their sweatshirts ride up, revealing a disturbing amount of buttock cleavage. Locally, this is called "crack."

Intermittently the men will emit unexpected ejaculations such as, "Holy Waugh!" or "Yah, sure, you betcha."

When you enter, all conversation will stop and all heads will swivel to see just what "foreigner" has entered their space.

There will be an ominous pause while they look over your L.L. Bean waffle-stompers and clean hiking pants with all the pockets; then the muttering will take on a disquieting tone. You won't quite be able to hear it, but this is what they are saying: "What do them trolls want? Are they gonna move up here and put up NO TRESPASSING signs on our favorite hunting spots? Soon, they'll be whining that their fancy cell phones don't work this far north and the shopping malls are too small."

Leon drifts over to where the locals are growling and reminds them to "Take it easy, guys. Remember, they're not just trolls from below the bridge, what they really are is income."

When Leon is summoned by other customers, Tyler Curnow twirls on his stool and adjusts his cap so that the large F.U. letters can be seen by the group of visitors. He's proud of the fact that he attended Finlandia University in Hancock for one semester, and even though he flunked out, he always wears the F.U. cap for its shock value.

Tyler breaks the silence, "But them folks could all stay home and just send us the money." Warming to the idea, Tyler continues with increasing enthusiasm, "We could work up a new interactive computer program that would provide a 'virtual U.P. experience.' Hey, there's programs like that for everything–virtual pets, space

travel, even virtual sex." After pausing to sip his beer, Tyler is now in full cry: "Picture it guys–a computer program with the sound of a winter blizzard, pictures and audio of an outhouse, the smell of a hot pasty… it could even dispense a deer turd!"

His two drinking buddies just nod but say nothing. They are very familiar with Tyler's enthusiasm for off-the-wall ideas;

they think he's still a good guy even though he doesn't have both oars in the water. They remember the time, when he had to dig a new pit for his outhouse and fill in the old one–a nasty job. He hinted all around town that Jimmy Hoffa might be buried on his property. He thought maybe the FBI might hear about it, come up to his place, dig around just like they excavated an entire farm in Lower Michigan. Presto, he'd have a new pit!

And then that baiting thing during deer season. That was weird, even for Tyler. While other hunters put out apples and corn to attract deer, Tyler baited with Godiva chocolate. He said he was tired of sitting out in the woods year after year, getting cold and and looking for bucks. He hoped that, instead of deer, he could lure Pamela Anderson, Catherine Zeta-Jones or Heather Locklear to his deer blind.

Don't you think it would be better for you to have a chicken dinner in Frankenmuth or a slice of cherry pie in Traverse City?

Epilogue

THE LAST NOTE SAM SATTERLY left for me was pinned to a white pine tree beside Foster Creek on the eastern edge of our homestead. Paraphrasing Chief Joseph of the Nez Perce, Sam wrote, "From where the sun sets, I shall write no more forever."

Well, that goes for me too, Sam. However, those of us who live on and love this beautiful peninsula are alarmed at the swift and terrible march of exploitation by those who wish to convert this land into cash as fast as possible. And so, once again I offer this plea:

> *Please don't come to the Upper Peninsula and try to alter the land or our way of life. Don't set about to change this place into the place you have just left (or fled).*

It is what it Is and we like it that way.

Rather, approach our beloved north country with reverence and awe.

Tuck yourself in here and let the land change you.

ABOUT THE Author

LON EMERICK is a fifth-generation descendant of Cornish copper miners who came to the region in the mid-l800s. As a disciple of Henry David Thoreau, he explores and writes about the woods and waters of the Superior Peninsula.

In a prior lifetime, Emerick was a professor of speech pathology at several universities, with the longest and most satisfying years at Northern Michigan University. Although he is the author of several textbooks and numerous professional articles in speech pathology, he is pleased to be most identified with his later books about his ancestral land–the Upper Peninsula of Michigan.

Lon Emerick lives now with his wife Lynn in a log home in the woods of West Branch Township, Marquette County.

CREDITS AND Acknowledgements

The author and publisher acknowledge, with special thanks, permissions granted for use of original images, photographs and writings.

Front cover photograph: *End of Earth*. Adapted from a sign and photograph created by John A. Marchesi and Tim Cocciolone. © John A. Marchesi, 1985. Used by permission.

Map of the Real U.P. created by Eugene Sinervo © Eugene S. Sinervo, 1972. Used by permission: Vincent Sinervo

Back cover photo: *Author Lon Emerick with Sam Satterly's birchbark notes, at roadside mailbox.* Photo credit: Lynn McGlothlin

The quote by Heather Lende, from *If You Lived Here, I'd Know Your Name.* Algonquin Books, 2005, is reprinted by permission.

For the concept of "disturbing illustrations"–*Uncle Mike's Guide to the Real Oregon Coast* by Mike Burgess, illustrated by Steve McLeod. Left Coast Group, no date.

Lon Emerick books available from
North Country Publishing:
(including those which so distressed Sam Satterly)

The Superior Peninsula: Seasons in the Upper Peninsula of Michigan
Merit award winner
Midwest Publishers Association

Going Back to Central: On the Road in Search of the Past in Michigan's Upper Peninsula
A Library of Michigan Notable Book
Best in Travel Books,
Midwest Publishers Association

Sharing the Journey: Lessons from my Students and Clients with Tangled Tongues

Other Lon Emerick books by Avery Color Studios:

You Wouldn't Like It Here–
A Guide to the Real Upper
Peninsula of Michigan
Humor Finalist - Foreword
Book of the Year Awards